CONTE

RECIPE

BRUMMIE BACON CAKES

These make a tasty and filling breakfast dish.

> 50g/2oz streaky bacon
> 225g/8oz self-raising flour
> Half a teaspoonful salt
> 25g/1oz butter or margarine
> 75g/3oz grated Cheddar cheese
> 150ml/ ¼ pint milk
> 1 tablespoonful tomato ketchup
> A dash of Worcestershire Sauce, to taste
> Milk for glazing

Pre-heat the oven to 200°C/400°F/Gas Mark 6. Grill the bacon until crisp, and chop it into small pieces. Sieve the flour and salt into a bowl and rub in the butter or margarine until the mixture resembles fine breadcrumbs. Add the chopped bacon and one third of the cheese. Mix the milk, ketchup and Worcestershire Sauce together in a separate bowl. Add the dry ingredients, and mix together well to make a soft dough. Roll out on a floured board into a circle about 18-20cm (7-8 inches) in diameter. Brush the top with milk and cut the dough into 8 wedges. Arrange the wedges on a greased baking sheet and sprinkle with the remaining cheese. Bake in the pre-heated oven for about 30 minutes until crisp.

Flavours of...

BIRMINGHAM & WEST MIDLANDS

RECIPES

Compiled by Julia Skinner

THE FRANCIS FRITH COLLECTION

www.francisfrith.com

First published in the United Kingdom in 2011 by The Francis Frith Collection®

This edition published exclusively for Identity Books in 2011 ISBN 978-1-84589-554-9

Text and Design copyright The Francis Frith Collection®
Photographs copyright The Francis Frith Collection® except where indicated.

The Frith® photographs and the Frith® logo are reproduced under licence from
Heritage Photographic Resources Ltd, the owners of the Frith® archive and trademarks.
'The Francis Frith Collection', 'Francis Frith' and 'Frith' are registered trademarks of
Heritage Photographic Resources Ltd.

All rights reserved. No photograph in this publication may be sold to a third party other than in the original
form of this publication, or framed for sale to a third party. No parts of this publication may be reproduced,
stored in a retrieval system, or transmitted, in any form, or by any means, electronic, mechanical, photocopying,
recording or otherwise, without the prior permission of the publishers and copyright holder.

British Library Cataloguing in Publication Data

Flavours of Birmingham & West Midlands - Recipes
Compiled by Julia Skinner

The Francis Frith Collection
Unit 6, Oakley Business Park,
Wylye Road, Dinton,
Wiltshire SP3 5EU
Tel: +44 (0) 1722 716 376
Email: info@francisfrith.co.uk
www.francisfrith.com

Printed and bound in England

Front Cover: **BIRMINGHAM, VICTORIA SQUARE AND THE COUNCIL HOUSE
c1960** B100050p

Frontispiece: **BIRMINGHAM, THE MUSEUM AND ART GALLERY c1960** B100048

The colour-tinting is for illustrative purposes only, and is not intended to be historically accurate

AS WITH ANY HISTORICAL DATABASE, THE FRANCIS FRITH ARCHIVE IS CONSTANTLY BEING
CORRECTED AND IMPROVED, AND THE PUBLISHERS WOULD WELCOME INFORMATION ON
OMISSIONS OR INACCURACIES

BIRMINGHAM, NEW STREET
1890 B10000lz

BIRMINGHAM, THE INDUSTRIAL PIONEERS MEMORIAL BROAD STREET c1960 B100052

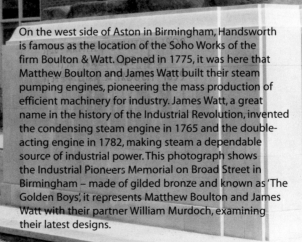

On the west side of Aston in Birmingham, Handsworth is famous as the location of the Soho Works of the firm Boulton & Watt. Opened in 1775, it was here that Matthew Boulton and James Watt built their steam pumping engines, pioneering the mass production of efficient machinery for industry. James Watt, a great name in the history of the Industrial Revolution, invented the condensing steam engine in 1765 and the double-acting engine in 1782, making steam a dependable source of industrial power. This photograph shows the Industrial Pioneers Memorial on Broad Street in Birmingham – made of gilded bronze and known as 'The Golden Boys', it represents Matthew Boulton and James Watt with their partner William Murdoch, examining their latest designs.

BIRMINGHAM SOUP

The 1790s in England were a time of poor harvests and high food prices, and a number of soup kitchens were set up to provide cheap, nourishing food for those in need. One of those concerned about the plight of the poor was Matthew Boulton, of the Birmingham firm Boulton & Watt (see opposite). Birmingham Archives and Heritage Service holds an extensive collection of Matthew Boulton's papers, and in one of his notebooks, dated 1793, is his handwritten recipe for Birmingham Soup, to be sold at one penny a quart (2 pints, or 1.2 litres). This is a modern adaptation of Boulton's recipe. It is surprisingly good, rather like Scotch Broth, and makes a hearty broth for a cold winter's day.

> 450g/1 lb lean stewing or braising beef, or shin of beef
> 1.2 litres/2 pints water, or beef stock
> 50g/2oz Quick Soup Mix (a mix of split peas, pearl barley, lentils and oatflakes that does not need to be soaked before using, available from supermarkets or health food shops)
> *Alternatively, use 25g/1oz dried peas, soaked in water overnight, and 25g/1oz pearl barley, soaked in water for 2 hours, if preferred – as in the original recipe*
> 1 medium sized onion, peeled and chopped
> 1 small turnip, peeled and diced into very small pieces
> 1 large carrot, peeled and diced into very small pieces
> 1 medium sized potato, peeled and diced into very small pieces
> 2 tablespoonfuls medium oatmeal
> Salt and pepper to taste
> One slice of bread per person, with their crusts cut off
> Vegetable oil, or lard or dripping, for frying
> 1 tablespoonful chopped fresh parsley to garnish

Trim the meat, and cut it into very small pieces. Put the meat into a large saucepan with the Quick Soup Mix (or the soaked pearl barley and dried peas), and cover with 1.2 litres (2 pints) of cold water, or beef stock. Bring it slowly to the boil, skimming off the scum as it rises. Add the prepared vegetables, bring back to the boil, then reduce to a low heat, cover the pan and leave to simmer gently for 2½ hours. Mix the oatmeal to a paste with a little water and add to the broth. Bring it to the boil again, then season with salt and pepper, reduce the heat and simmer, uncovered, for a further 20 minutes, stirring occasionally as the soup thickens, so it does not stick to the bottom of the pan. The original recipe ends: *The Bread is cut in small pieces and put in when removed from the fire. The Bread is much better when fried in Lard or Dripping.* When the soup is ready to serve, cut the bread slices into small cubes. Heat some oil or dripping in a frying pan and fry the bread cubes for a minute or so, until they are crisp and golden on both sides. Serve the soup in individual bowls with the fried bread cubes thrown on top and a little finely chopped fresh parsley scattered over them.

RECIPE

ANGELS ON HORSEBACK

Photograph 37276 (opposite) shows Christ Church in 1896, which used to stand on the corner of Colmore Row and New Street in Birmingham. Christ Church was closed and demolished in 1899 to make way for a new block of shops and offices, and the Church of St Agatha in Sparkbrook was erected to replace it. The group of people seen on the bottom right of this photograph, at the road level below the railings around the forecourt of the church, are standing outside Arthur Moore's Oyster Rooms, which was the first shop beneath Christ Church at the top of New Street. This recipe was a popular snack in Victorian times and makes a delicious snack or appetizer. It was included in the 1888 edition of 'Mrs Beeton's Book of Household Management' – just a few years before our photograph was taken. Perhaps it was served in Moore's Oyster Rooms!

> 16 oysters, removed from their shells
> Fresh lemon juice
> 8 rashers of streaky bacon with their rinds removed
> 8 small slices of bread
> Butter
> Paprika, or a dash of Tabasco sauce (optional)

Pre-heat the oven to 200°C/400°C/Gas Mark 6.

Sprinkle each oyster with a little lemon juice. Lay the bacon rashers on a board, slide the back of a knife along each one to stretch it and then cut it in half crosswise. Wrap a piece of bacon around each oyster and secure with a wooden cocktail stick. Arrange the bacon-wrapped oysters on a baking sheet. Put the oysters and bacon into the pre-heated hot oven and cook for 8-10 minutes. Whilst the bacon and oysters are cooking, toast the bread. When the bacon is cooked through, spread each slice of hot toast with butter, and place a bacon-wrapped oyster on top of each piece. Sprinkle with a little paprika or a dash of Tabasco sauce, if used, before serving.

BIRMINGHAM
CHRIST CHURCH 1896
37276

STILL AT THE FRONT!

ALBION LAMP COMPANY BIRMINGHAM

THE "ALBIONETTE"

In all the industrial towns of the West Midlands in the past, where money was sometimes short, people made the best possible use of economical cuts of meat and many traditional dishes evolved using offal, off-cuts and cheap parts of the animal. These dishes included cow heel jelly, pigs' trotters, chitterlings, tripe and onions (see page 17), haslet (a meat loaf that is eaten cold, cut into slices) and faggots, which were often called 'Poor Man's Goose' in many parts of England. Faggots are still very popular in the West Midlands. Homemade faggots are very nutritious, and the recipe on the opposite page is a modernised version that brings the dish up to date with a special gravy. If mincing up all the meat yourself does not appeal, ask your butcher to do it for you.

RECIPE

FAGGOTS WITH ONION AND RED WINE GRAVY

For the faggots:
25g/1oz unsalted butter
1 medium onion, peeled and
   finely chopped
175g/6oz minced pigs' liver
2 lambs' or pigs' hearts, trimmed
   and cut into chunks
450g/1 lb belly pork, trimmed
   and rind removed
Half a teaspoonful of ground
   mace
4 tablespoonfuls freshly
   chopped chives
1 teaspoonful freshly chopped
   sage leaves
1 egg, beaten

Salt and freshly ground pepper
115g/4oz fresh white bread
   crumbs
25g/1oz beef dripping or 3
   tablespoonfuls olive oil

For the gravy:
4 red onions, peeled, and with
   each onion cut into 8 wedges
4 sprigs of fresh thyme
1 tablespoonful olive oil
900ml/1½ pints fresh beef stock
300ml/ ½ pint red wine
Salt and freshly ground black
   pepper

Melt the butter in a small saucepan and add the onions. Cook until soft and transparent, then leave to cool slightly. Place the belly pork onto a chopping board and cut into portions. Place the minced liver into a large glass bowl and place under the blade of a mincer. Using a fine blade of a mincer, mince the pork belly and hearts directly into the bowl with the liver. Add the cooled chopped onions, mace, chives, sage, beaten egg and salt and pepper. Stir in the breadcrumbs. Using your hands, shape the mixture into 12 patties. Place them on a plate and chill in the fridge for about 1 hour.

Pre-heat the oven to 200°C/400°F/Gas Mark 6, then place the onion wedges into a large roasting pan or ovenproof dish. Add the thyme and drizzle over the olive oil. Place in the oven and roast uncovered for 40 minutes until the onions are caramelised. Meanwhile heat the dripping or olive oil in a large frying pan. Fry the faggots until golden brown on both sides. Place the stock and wine in a small saucepan, bring to the boil and reduce by a third. Remove the roasted onions from the oven and lay the faggots on top. Pour over the gravy liqueur. Reduce the oven temperature to 180°C/350°F/Gas Mark 4 and cook the faggots in the oven for 40 minutes. Place two to three faggots onto a plate. Top with a spoonful of the onions and pour over the gravy. Serve the faggots with mashed potatoes and green vegetables, particularly peas, which are the traditional accompaniment to faggots.

CHICKEN LEGS IN BARBECUE SAUCE

The recipe for the famous spicy HP brown sauce was invented in the late 19th century by Frederick Gibson Garton in his pickling factory in Nottingham. Mr Garton sold the recipe and brand name for £150 to his vinegar supplier, Samson Moore of the Midland Vinegar Company at Aston Cross in Birmingham, to settle an outstanding debt, and Mr Moore launched HP Sauce commercially in 1903, to great success. Tradition says that Mr Garton named his sauce 'HP' as he had heard it was being served in a restaurant in the Houses of Parliament. HP Sauce continued to be made at the Aston factory until 2007 when production of the sauce was (controversially) moved to the Netherlands by Heinz, who purchased HP Foods in 2005, and the Aston factory was demolished. This easy recipe may not be *haute cuisine* but it recalls the proud place of HP Sauce in Birmingham's culinary heritage by using it to make a spicy barbecue sauce that goes well with chicken, sausages and burgers. Any leftover sauce can be kept to be used cold, as a tasty relish. This amount serves 4-8 people, depending on appetite.

> 50g/2oz butter
> 1 medium onion, finely chopped
> 1 clove of garlic, crushed or finely chopped
> 1 x 400g (16oz) can of chopped tomatoes, and the juice
> 2 tablespoonfuls of HP Sauce
> 1 tablespoonful of runny honey
> Salt and pepper to taste
> 8 chicken drumsticks
> Enough long-grain rice to serve 4 people

Combine the butter, chopped onions, garlic, tomatoes and their juice, HP Sauce, honey, and plenty of salt and pepper in a saucepan. Bring to the boil then reduce the heat to low, then gently simmer the sauce for about 30 minutes (uncovered) until it has thickened slightly, stirring occasionally to prevent it sticking to the bottom of the pan.

Whilst the sauce is cooking, cook the rice and then keep it hot whilst you prepare the chicken drumsticks.

Pre-heat the grill to hot. Place the chicken drumsticks in the grill pan and brush them liberally with the barbecue sauce. Grill the chicken drumsticks for 10 minutes on each side, brushing frequently with more sauce. Serve the chicken on a bed of cooked rice, with extra sauce spooned over them.

BIRMINGHAM, CORPORATION STREET 1890 B100002x

THE BALTI TRIANGLE

Present-day Birmingham is a vibrant, multi-cultural city and is renowned for its wide range of excellent restaurants serving cuisine from all over the world. It is especially famous for its superb Asian restaurants, particularly its balti restaurants in the so-called 'Balti Triangle' of the Sparkbrook, Balsall Heath and Ladypool areas of the city.

A balti is a spicy aromatic dish originally devised in the Sparkbrook area of Birmingham in the 1970s by residents from the Pakistani Kashmiri community who were unhappy with the oily food available in the area at the time. It is cooked in a special flat-bottomed two-handled cooking pot made of thin steel, which heats up quickly when placed over a flame and allows food to be cooked very swiftly using the stir-fry process, which retains the goodness and flavour of the food and spices whilst using very little oil. The food is both cooked and served to the table in the cooking pot, also called a 'balti', and thus the name of the cooking utensil has also become the name of the dish that is cooked in it. A true balti cooked in a proper balti pan is made with meat and vegetables such as tomatoes, onions, ginger and garlic, and authentic, best quality, freshly ground spices, combined with herbs like coriander, fenugreek and mint. A good balti has a distinctive fresh flavour, where the dish is not overpowered by heat or spice. A well-prepared authentic balti is a work of art and a definite gastronomic experience. A balti is traditionally not served with rice but with large naan bread pieces.

Many Asian restaurants around the country claim to make and serve the dish, but you only get an authentic balti in Birmingham. In recent years members of Birmingham City Council have considered applying for the balti to be given PDO (Protected Destination of Origin) and PGI (Protected Geographical Indication) status, to ensure that only dishes made in Birmingham can carry the name. Supporters of the proposal say the balti was created in one particular area by members of a specific community at a particular time, and the inferior concoctions served in curry houses elsewhere are nothing like a good Birmingham balti. If it doesn't come from Brum, then it isn't a true balti!

**BIRMINGHAM
CHAMBERLAIN SQUARE
c1960** B100047

**SUTTON COLDFIELD
THE PARADE 1949** S339006

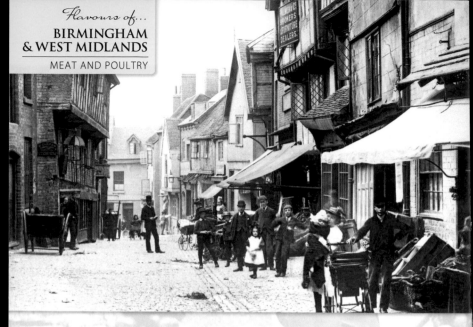

COVENTRY, BUTCHER'S ROW 1892 30916A

Birmingham was formerly in Warwickshire. In 1974 a 'new' county called West Midlands was created, which comprised parts of Staffordshire, Worcestershire and Warwickshire, including Birmingham and other places formerly in Warwickshire such as Sutton Coldfield, Solihull and Coventry. A dish that was traditionally very popular all over what is now West Midlands was tripe and onions. Many people nowadays are averse to the thought of eating tripe, but tripe was commonly eaten in the past and for those who like it, it is a very good dish, succulent in texture. Tripe is the edible stomach linings of an ox or cow. The first lining is called 'blanket', the second 'honeycomb' and the third 'double' or 'thick seam'. The appearance of the three linings is different, but they all taste the same. There are a number of traditional methods of preparing tripe, but one of the favourite methods is that given on the opposite page, plain and simple, with the tripe slow-cooked with onions for several hours, simmered in milk which is then used to make a rich creamy sauce to accompany it.

RECIPE

TRIPE AND ONIONS

Tripe is not often found in supermarkets, so you will probably need to get the tripe from a traditional butcher, if you are lucky enough to still have one in your area – use them or lose them! Ask for a mixture of all the different parts of tripe for this dish. This amount is enough for 4 people.

450g/1 lb best prepared and dressed tripe, washed
3 large onions, peeled and sliced
550ml/1 pint milk
25g/1oz butter
25g/1oz plain flour
1 bay leaf
A pinch of freshly grated nutmeg
1 level teaspoonful of dry mustard powder
Salt and freshly ground black pepper
1 rounded tablespoonful of finely chopped fresh parsley

Place the tripe in a saucepan and cover with lightly salted cold water. Bring to the boil, then remove from the heat, drain the tripe and rinse it under cold running water. Cut the tripe into 2.5cm (1 inch) pieces. Put a layer of the onions in the rinsed-out pan, then the tripe, then the rest of the onions. Pour in the milk, and add the bayleaf, the freshly grated nutmeg and just a pinch of salt. Put the pan on a medium heat and bring the milk very slowly to just below the boil, then reduce the heat to very low, cover the pan with its lid and leave to simmer gently for as long as possible, until the tripe is very tender – at least 2 hours, longer if you can. Stir occasionally to prevent any sticking. When the tripe is ready, remove the pan from the heat and strain it, reserving the cooking liquid. Measure the liquid, and make it up to 550ml (1 pint) with more milk if necessary. Keep the tripe and onions warm whilst you make the sauce. Melt the butter in a saucepan, stir in the flour and the mustard powder, and allow it to cook gently for 2-3 minutes, stirring, then gradually blend in the tripe cooking liquid, a little at a time, stirring constantly as you bring the sauce to the boil and it thickens. Reduce the heat and add the tripe and onions to the sauce, then simmer the mixture for 10 minutes, without allowing it to boil. Turn out the tripe and onions into a warmed serving bowl and garnish with finely chopped fresh parsley. Serve immediately, piping hot, with potatoes and seasonal vegetables.

THE BLACK COUNTRY

Also now part of the 'new' county of West Midlands is the Black Country, an area taken from parts of Staffordshire and Worcestershire. A common definition of the Black Country encompasses most of the Metropolitan Boroughs of Dudley, Sandwell, Walsall and the City of Wolverhampton. An alternative geological definition follows the outcroppings of the South Staffordshire 'thick' coal seam, and on this definition the outcropping of the coal seams near Halesowen and Stourbridge provides a southern boundary. Within this definition, parts of Walsall, Wolverhampton and Stourbridge are not within the Black Country, but West Bromwich is. The name 'Black Country' probably derived from the smoke and dirt of what was for many centuries an area of heavy industrialisation. Descriptions of this region in the 17th and 18th centuries often describe scenes of a 'hell on earth', and Thomas Carlyle (1795-1881) wrote of 'a frightful scene (with) a dense cloud of pestilential smoke (where) the whole region burns like a volcano spitting fire from a thousand tubes of brick'. Dudley is traditionally seen as the capital of the Black Country. Exploitation of Dudley's natural resources began well before the Industrial Revolution and the town centre became the site of many industries, most of which were in the Black Country tradition of 'metal bashing', notably that of fender and fire-iron manufacture.

For many years the name 'Black Country' was almost a term of disparagement, describing a hardworking but unattractive area, but in recent times the growth of the tourist industry has turned it into a powerful marketing tool that is used and borne with pride. The region's industrial past has now become something of great interest, and the superb Black Country Living Museum in Dudley is a popular visitor attraction. Another way in which Dudley celebrates its proud industrial heritage is with the sculptured frieze in the town centre. Installed in 1963, it depicts, at each end, the area's traditional industries of chain-making and coal-mining, with a mother and child in the centre representing education. The section shown on the opposite page is the chain-maker.

DUDLEY, PART OF THE SCULPTURE FRIEZE, BIRDCAGE WALK
c1965 D103123x

DUDLEY, HIGH STREET AND THE PARISH CHURCH c1955 D103036

RECIPE

BLACK COUNTRY BEEF STEW

450g/1 lb stewing steak
300ml/ ½ pint mild ale
300ml/ ½ pint beef stock
225g/8oz black pudding, sliced
115g/4oz mushrooms
2 large onions
1 tablespoonful tomato purée
1 teaspoonful parsley, finely chopped
Half a teaspoonful sage, finely chopped
Half a teaspoonful thyme, finely chopped
1 bay leaf
Salt and pepper
Oil for frying

Slice the onions and dice the steak. Heat a little oil in a medium-sized saucepan and fry the onions until softened. Add the diced steak a few pieces at a time and lightly brown.

Add the ale, tomato purée and the chopped fresh herbs and the bay leaf, and season to taste. Simmer gently for 20 minutes to reduce slightly, then add the stock and simmer for 1½ hours.

Fry the slices of black pudding and mushrooms, and add to the stew. Return the stew to the boil briefly, then serve with new potatoes and green vegetables.

WOLVERHAMPTON, DUDLEY STREET
c1900 W285007

RECIPE

GROATY PUDDING

One of the most popular vegetables found in gardens and allotments in the West Midlands is the leek. A highlight for vegetable growers in the area is the Annual Horticultural and Midland Leek Show which is part of the Sandwell Community Show held every August in Sandwell, a metropolitan borough made up of the towns of Oldbury, Rowley Regis, Smethwick, Tipton, Wednesbury, Cradley Heath, Tividale and West Bromwich. The Midland Leek Show attracts competitors from throughout the region, and gives growers the chance to win much-coveted prizes for their giant vegetables. However, for cooking purposes it is better to use smaller leeks! Leeks are one of the ingredients of Groaty Pudding (or Groaty Dick), a traditional dish from the Black Country that was often served on Bonfire Night. Groats are whole grains of oats with the husks removed, but before they have been ground to produce oatmeal, or rolled to make rolled oats; they are not the same thing as jumbo whole rolled oats that you can buy for making porridge. If groats prove hard to find, they can be bought over the internet, or try looking in health food shops or even pet food suppliers – they are often sold as bird food.

> 450g/1 lb stewing beef or shin of beef
> 2 onions, peeled and finely chopped
> 2 leeks, trimmed, washed and finely sliced
> 225g/8oz oat groats
> 1 bayleaf
> Salt and pepper to taste
> Enough boiling water or hot beef stock to cover
>   ingredients in cooking pot

Pre-heat the oven to 150°C/300°F/Gas Mark 2. Trim the meat and cut it into bite-sized pieces. Put the meat, the prepared onions and leeks and the bayleaf into a large ovenproof dish (preferably an earthenware one). Season to taste with salt and pepper. Pour in enough boiling water or hot beef stock to cover the ingredients. Cover the dish with its lid and cook in the pre-heated oven for at least 3 hours, or longer if you can. The groats will absorb the cooking liquid and expand, thickening the stew. Serve with potatoes, or crusty bread if preferred – in the past, Groaty Pudding was often served spread on slices of bread.

WILLENHALL, MARKET PLACE c1965 W238010

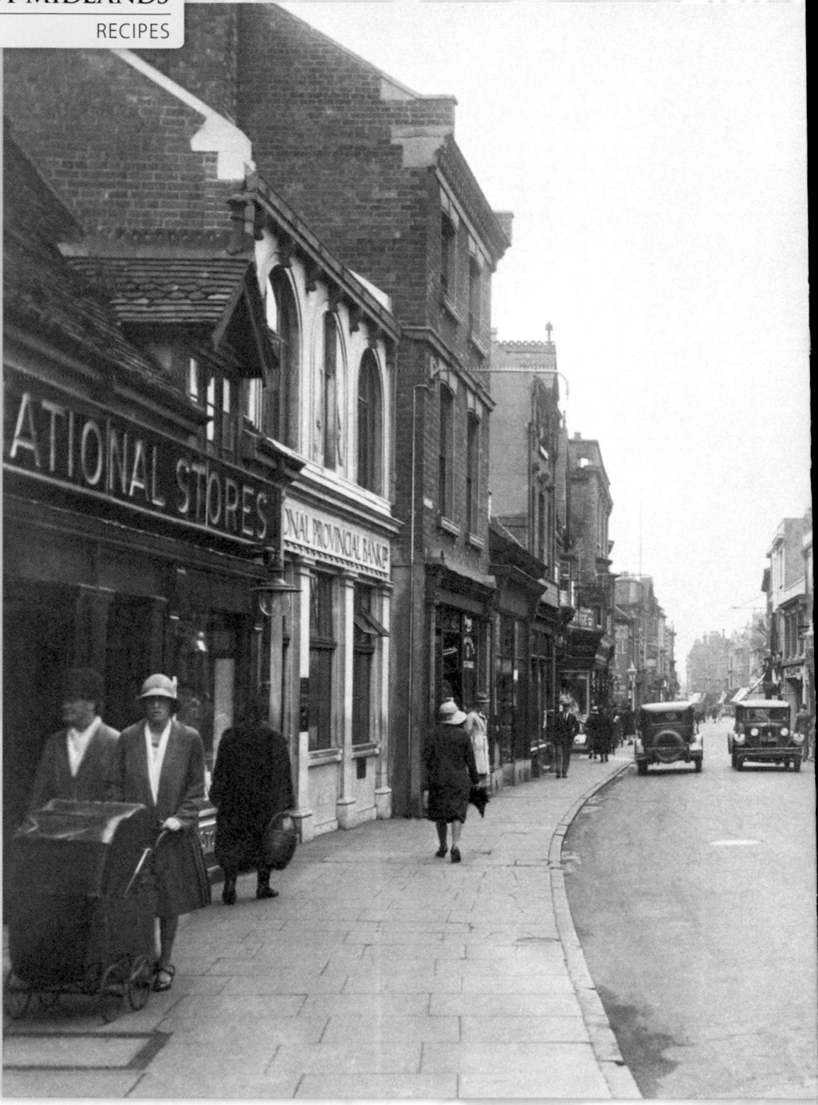
ATIONAL STORES
ONAL PROVINCIAL BANK

STOURBRIDGE, HIGH STREET 1931 84685

RECIPE

CHEESE, ONION AND POTATO PIE

At the south of the borough of Solihull is the small village of Earlswood, which straddles the county border of Warwickshire and West Midlands. Earlswood is the home of Fowlers of Earlswood, the oldest family cheese-making firm in the country. Their range of traditional handcrafted cheeses can be found in supermarkets and Fowlers are also regular stallholders at the Birmingham City Centre Farmers Market, held on the first and third Wednesdays of each month in New Street. Their range includes cheeses flavoured with garlic and parsley, chilli, sage, cracked black pepper, onion and chives, and real ale and mustard. Why not use your own favourite Fowlers cheese in this savoury pie.

> 225g/8oz potatoes
> 75g/3oz hard cheese of choice, grated
> 1 small onion, very finely chopped
> 25g/1oz butter or margarine
> Salt and pepper
> 80ml/3fl oz milk
> 1 dessertspoonful chopped fresh parsley

Boil the potatoes until they soften. Melt half the butter or margarine in a pan and fry the chopped onion until it is soft and golden. Drain the cooked potatoes. Add the milk and remaining butter or margarine to the potatoes, season to taste and mash well until smooth.

Add the cooked onion, all but 2 tablespoonfuls of the grated cheese and the parsley to the mashed potatoes and mix it all together well. Put the mixture into a warmed shallow ovenproof dish, and smooth the top. Sprinkle the rest of the melted cheese on top, and brown under a hot grill before serving.

As a variation to this recipe, before sprinkling the cheese on the top of the pie, make four hollows on the top of the pie (by pressing the back of a spoon into the topping), and drop an egg into each hollow, topped with a small dot of butter. Sprinkle the grated cheese between the eggs, and bake in the pre-heated oven at 190°C/375°F/Gas Mark 5 for about 15-20 minutes, until the eggs have set.

**SOLIHULL, THE CLOCK TOWER
AND THE BARLEY MOW c1965**
S257085

THE BIRMINGHAM ONION FAIR

Despite the modern development that has taken place in Birmingham, the Bull Ring is still the centre of the city. It used to be the venue for an important annual event, the famous Birmingham Onion Fair, which celebrated the onion harvest in the autumn. This account of the Fair appeared in 'The Illustrated London News' in October 1872:

'The greatest manufacturing town of the Midland shires has retained a considerable trade in the agricultural produce of the surrounding country…But the unique feature of this particular aspect of Birmingham, as an agricultural market, is the Michaelmas Onion Fair. It is held on the last Thursday in September, in the wide open place called the Bull Ring, which is situated in the centre of town, in front of St. Martin's Church. This growth of this savoury vegetable is the object of much attention by many of the neighbouring market-gardeners and farmers, who find the soil and climate well adapted to its cultivation. Nowhere can such large quantities be seen or of finer quality, than in the special Fair at Birmingham, which took place as usual on Thursday week. The onions are piled in stacks, heaped in wooden crates or wicker baskets, spread upon wide stalls, or suspended in perpendicular ropes from cross-poles overhead, in the variety of arrangement for effective display. The air is fully charged with their pungent odour, causing the unaccustomed eye, perhaps, to shed an involuntary tear, while engaged in the inspection of their diverse kinds, though not a sorry sight. The dealers and customers at this Fair are mostly the country folk of Warwickshire, with a few tradesmen of the town and some of the workmen's wives for the onion gives a palatable relish to a poor man's dinner or supper.'

The sale of onions at the Fair in the past was accompanied by stalls, sideshows and amusements, and special excursion trains were run to the event from all over the area. However, after 1875 the onions and the amusements side of the Fair parted company. The amusements went to Aston and developed into a modern funfair, whilst the once-famous Onion Fair in the city centre for the sale of 'the savoury vegetable' is now just a part of Birmingham's history.

BIRMINGHAM, VICTORIA SQUARE AND THE COUNCIL HOUSE c1960 B100050

RECIPES

Here are two onion recipes recalling the importance of this vegetable to Birmingham in the past, when it was sold in huge quantities at the city's famous Onion Fair (see page 30). One recipe is for a traditional onion gravy, the other is for onion bhajis, linking Birmingham's past with its multi-cultural population of present times, and celebrating the modern city's reputation as a centre of Asian cuisine. Onion bhajis are savoury Asian snacks that have become popular all over Britain. They are small patties or balls made of sliced onions and flour, flavoured with spices and deep fried. There are many recipe variations, but they are very easy to make. They should properly be made with chick pea or gram flour which is available from Asian food stores, but if this is hard to find you can use plain flour instead. They can be eaten either as a snack on their own, or as a starter or side dish to a curry – try serving them with mango chutney or with a cucumber and mint raita (made by adding finely chopped cucumber and fresh mint leaves to natural yogurt).

ONION GRAVY

Onion gravy is a traditional delicacy that is still popular, and is particularly good served with sausages.

> 2 tablespoonfuls vegetable oil
> 1 large onion, halved then sliced
> 1 tablespoonful plain flour
> 360ml/12fl oz chicken stock
> 1 teaspoonful chopped mixed herbs, fresh or dried
> 1 teaspoonful Worcestershire Sauce

Heat the oil in a medium sized saucepan. Add the onions and sauté for about 10 minutes, until brown. Sprinkle the flour over the onions and continue to cook, stirring gently, for 2-3 minutes. Gradually add the stock, herbs and Worcestershire Sauce and continue to cook until thickened, stirring all the time. Partially cover and cook for a further 10-15 minutes to allow the flavours to develop, stirring from time to time.

ONION BHAJIS (ONION BHAJIAS)

Onion bhajis should be mildly spicy, not hot, but increase the amounts of spices in this recipe if you prefer their flavour to be more prominent. This amount makes about 16 small onion bhajis, or about 8 larger ones.

115g/4oz chick pea flour or gram flour (or use plain flour instead, if this is hard to find)
1 teaspoonful Garam Masala, or curry powder
Half a teaspoonful chilli powder
Half a teaspoonful ground turmeric
Half a teaspoonful ground cumin
Half a teaspoonful baking powder
Salt to taste
1 large onion or 2 medium onions, peeled, cut into halves and then finely sliced into long thin strands
1 green chilli, deseeded and finely chopped
1 tablespoonful mango chutney
1 heaped tablespoonful finely chopped fresh coriander leaves
A small amount of cold water, for mixing
Vegetable oil, for deep frying

Sift the flour, Garam Masala or curry powder, chilli powder, turmeric, cumin, baking powder and salt into a large mixing bowl. Add the onion slices, chopped chilli, mango chutney and chopped coriander leaves, and mix it all together well. Gradually add a little water to the flour mixture, just enough to combine it all together in a thick, stiff paste, and mix it until the onions are well coated. The mixture should not be runny, but should stick and hold together well. Leave the mixture to stand for 10 minutes for the flavours to develop. Heat the oil in a large pan or deep fat fryer to 180°/350°, or until a cube of bread browns quickly in it. When it is ready, drop spoonfuls of the mixture into the hot fat – about the size of an egg or a golf ball for small bhajis, or the size of a tennis ball for larger ones. Fry the bhajis in the hot oil in batches until they are crisp and golden brown on both sides; this should take about 3 minutes on each side for small bhajis, but longer for larger ones. Allow the oil to heat up again between each batch. Remove from the oil with a slotted spoon and drain well on kitchen paper. Either eat them straight away, hot and crisp, or store in an airtight container and eat cold. They can also be reheated in the oven to crisp them up and serve hot when needed.

RECIPE

GREY PEAS AND BACON

Grey Peas and Bacon is a dish from the Black Country that was often eaten on Bonfire Night. The proper peas to use are dried maple peas, also known as field peas or pigeon peas – they are often used as pigeon food, and can be bought from pet food suppliers if they prove hard to find. Maple peas are brown, but go grey when they are cooked, hence their name of 'grey peas'. If you can't find maple peas you can use black-eyed peas, dried green peas or even dried yellow split peas instead. Adding bicarbonate of soda to the water during the soaking process helps the peas to soften when they are cooked, but you can omit this if you prefer. Some people like to make this with just the peas and bacon, omitting the onion and pearl barley. The longer you leave this to cook, the better – the old Black Country tradition was 'soak for a day – cook for a day'!

> 450g/1 lb dried grey peas (or alternative, if they are hard to find – see above)
> 450g/1 lb bacon, chopped into small pieces
> 1 large onion, peeled and finely chopped
> 3oz/75g pearl barley
> Plenty of water for soaking the peas and barley
> 600ml/1 pint water or stock
> Oil for frying
> Pepper (you should not need to add salt, as the bacon will make the dish salty)
> 1 teaspoonful bicarbonate of soda

Wash the peas, put them in a large bowl, add the pearl barley and the bicarbonate of soda (if using), then put in enough water to cover them plus some on top, and leave to soak overnight. Next day, drain the peas and barley and rinse well. Heat a little oil in a large pan and fry the bacon pieces until browned and crispy. Add 600ml (1 pint) of water or stock, bring to the boil and add the soaked peas and barley and the chopped onion. Bring back to the boil and boil hard for 10 minutes, then cover the pan, reduce the heat to low and leave to simmer gently for at least 3 hours, longer if you can, topping up the pan now and again with more boiling water as necessary, until the peas are tender. Add a little salt to taste if necessary in the last half an hour of cooking. Serve with crusty bread.

**WOLVERHAMPTON
QUEEN STREET c1900** W285001

WEST BROMWICH, HIGH STREET 1963 W237003

RECIPE

FILL BELLY PUDDING

This is a traditional recipe from the Black Country that is also a good way of using up stale bread.

> 450g/1 lb stale bread
> 1 egg
> 115g/4oz suet
> 25g/1oz butter or margarine
> 225g/8oz granulated or brown sugar
> 1 level teaspoonful mixed spice
> 225g/8oz mixed dried fruit

Pre-heat the oven to 170°C/325°F/Gas Mark 3. Soak the bread in water for 10 minutes, then drain and squeeze out the excess moisture. Mash the bread with a fork, then add the remaining ingredients, mix well together and spread the mixture into a greased baking tin. Dot the surface with small knobs of butter, and bake in the pre-heated oven for about 2 hours, until nicely browned. Dredge some more sugar over the surface, and cut into squares to serve. This can be eaten either hot with custard or cream, or cold.

BRIERLEY HILL, HIGH STREET
c1965 B355017

CADBURY'S

"Afternoon Cocoa."

In enervating Summer weather something more is required than a drink that is only temporarily refreshing. CADBURY'S COCOA undoubtedly supplies the need—being a delicious, refreshing beverage; thin in fluid, highly nutritious, and most sustaining—repairing waste resulting from oppressive heat. It is a perfect drink and food combined.
☞ CADBURY'S is the ideal beverage for all times and seasons. It is absolutely Pure, therefore the Best Cocoa.

The famous Cadbury's chocolate business was started in Birmingham in 1824 when John Cadbury opened a shop at 93 Bull Street in the city centre to sell coffee, tea, cocoa and drinking chocolate. John Cadbury was a member of the Society of Friends, or Quakers as they were commonly called. Quakers were anti alcohol, seeing it as the cause of misery and deprivation in society, and John Cadbury offered his hot drinks as non-alcoholic alternatives for ordinary people. Situated just south of Birmingham is Bournville, which was chosen by John Cadbury's sons Richard and George Cadbury, also Quakers, in the late 19th century as the site for their new cocoa and chocolate factory and for a model village for their workers. Nowadays Bournville is the home of Cadbury World, where an exhibition tells the story of the history and manufacture of chocolate.

RECIPE

QUAKER'S CHOCOLATE PUDDING

115g/4oz butter or margarine
115g/4oz plain chocolate
150ml/ ¼ pint milk
115g/4oz fresh breadcrumbs
75g/3oz caster sugar
A few drops of vanilla essence
3 eggs, separated

Melt the butter or margarine with the chocolate in a small saucepan. Add the milk and the breadcrumbs, stir well and leave to cook gently for 10 minutes, stirring occasionally, then remove from heat and allow to cool slightly. Beat in the sugar and the vanilla essence, then beat the egg yolks into the chocolate mixture. Whisk the egg whites until they are stiff and stand in peaks, then fold them into the chocolate mixture, using a large metal spoon.

Grease a 1.2 litre (2 pint) pudding basin, and fill it with the pudding mixture. Cover the pudding basin with a lid of pleated greaseproof paper, and then another of foil, and tie down firmly with string. Place the pudding basin on a trivet or an upturned saucer in a large saucepan. Pour enough boiling water into the pan to come halfway up the sides of the basin. Place the pan on heat and bring the water back to the boil, then cover the pan with its lid and steam the pudding for about 1 hour, replenishing the pan with more boiling water when necessary, so that it does not boil dry.

When cooked, turn out the pudding on to a warmed serving dish, and serve with cream or chocolate sauce.

**BIRMINGHAM, THE TOWN HALL
AND PARADISE STREET 1896** 37274

RECITPE

PARADISE POTS

Celebrate Birmingham's chocolate heritage with these delicious chocolate fondant puddings with a meltingly gooey centre – a taste of paradise for chocolate lovers everywhere! This amount makes 4 servings.

125g/4½ oz butter, cut into small pieces
A little extra butter for greasing the ramekins
175g/6oz caster sugar
125g/4½ oz Bournville Classic dark chocolate
   (or a 70% dark chocolate of choice)
3 large eggs
40g/1½ oz plain flour (or 4½ level tablespoonfuls)
A little icing sugar or cocoa powder, to finish
Whipped or clotted cream, to serve.

Pre-heat the oven to 200°C/400°F/Gas Mark 6. Lightly butter the insides of four ramekin dishes, or other small individual ovenproof dishes, and coat the insides of each dish with a teaspoonful of the caster sugar. Break the chocolate into small pieces. Place the chocolate and butter pieces in a bowl and set it over a pan of hot water at a gentle simmering point until the butter and chocolate has all melted. Stir the mixture until it is smooth and glossy, then put to one side. Put the remaining sugar and the eggs into another bowl and beat together with a balloon whisk for one minute, then sift the flour on top of the mixture. Pour the chocolate mixture into the bowl, pouring it around the sides, then use a large metal spoon to fold the mixture together, gently but thoroughly, until you are left with a glossy brown sauce with no white streaks or floury lumps – take some time to do this properly, or you will have a stodgy sponge base at the bottom of your puddings. Pour the mixture into the ramekins, filling each one up to about 1cm (½ inch) from the top. Stand the ramekins on a baking tray and bake in the pre-heated oven for 15 minutes. Remove from the oven and leave to settle for 5 minutes before serving – you can eat them straight from the oven, but the centres of the puddings will be very runny, and leaving them for a few minutes allows the chocolate sauce inside them to thicken a little. Finish by sifting a little icing sugar or cocoa powder over them before serving with a dollop of whipped or clotted cream on top of each pudding. For special occasions dress them up even more, by decorating the cream with a raspberry or two and a mint leaf.

RECIPE

BILBERRY AND APPLE PIE

Eleven miles south-west of the centre of Birmingham are the Lickey Hills, a country park area in Worcestershire. 'The Lickeys' and much of the area around Rednall would have been built on in the 1880s, had it not been for the intervention of the Birmingham Association for the Preservation of Open Spaces. They managed to save 32 acres of countryside from the developers, and the land was later acquired by the Birmingham Corporation and opened to the public. Edward and George Cadbury of Bournville provided additional funds for the purchase of the adjoining Bilberry Hill, which is named after the extensive tracts of bilberry bushes (Vaccinium myrtillus) that grow over much of the hill. For hundreds of years, local people and visitors to the area have cropped the bushes of their free fruit each autumn, to make jams, preserves or bilberry pies. Bilberries grow on small bushes close to the ground and are hard work to pick, but are worth the effort. If you don't want to pick your own bilberries to make this pie, use commercially grown blueberries instead.

450g/1 lb bilberries (or blueberries)
2 cooking apples
225g/8oz sugar
1 egg, beaten
350g/12oz sweet shortcrust or puff pastry, whichever is preferred

Heat the oven to 200°C/400°F/Gas Mark 6. Remove the cores from the apples with an apple corer, but do not peel them. Stand the apples in an ovenproof dish, add 2 tablespoonfuls of water to the dish and bake in the pre-heated oven for 40-45 minutes, until the apples are tender. When cooked, scrape out the pulp from the apples and mix it with the bilberries and the sugar. Roll out half the pastry on a lightly floured board and use it to line a greased 20cm (8 inch) pie tin. Turn out the fruit mixture into the pie tin. Roll out the remaining pastry to make a lid and place it over the pie, and trim and seal the edges. Brush the lid of the pie with beaten egg white and sprinkle with sugar. Place in the pre-heated oven and bake for ten minutes, then reduce the heat to 180°/350°C/Gas Mark 4 and cook for a further 30 minutes until the pastry is golden brown and crisp.

BIRD'S CUSTARD

A favourite accompaniment to a pudding or pie is custard. Proper custard is made with eggs, but in the 1830s Alfred Bird invented an egg-free cornflour-based powder which thickens to form a custard-like sauce when mixed with milk, which he devised because his wife was allergic to eggs. His product became popular, and he formed a company to make and sell what is now famous as Bird's Custard powder from a factory in Birmingham. The Bird's Custard brand is now owned by Premier Foods and production of the custard powder was relocated to Banbury in Oxfordshire in 1964, but Alfred Bird's large factory that was built in 1904 in the Digbeth area of Birmingham, where around 1,000 people once worked, still stands in the city, now converted into an arts centre called The Custard Factory in Gibb Street. Another memento of the Bird family is the statue known as 'The Prancing Horse and Man' in Malvern Park in Solihull, shown in photograph S257045, below. Sculpted by Sir Joseph Edgar Boehm, it was bought and donated to Solihull by Captain Oliver Bird, grandson of Alfred Bird, in 1944.

SOLIHULL, THE STATUE IN MALVERN PARK c1965 S257045

Flavours of...
**BIRMINGHAM
& WEST MIDLANDS**
PUDDINGS, PIES & DESSERTS

F.W.WOOLWORTH & C°

RECIPE

GOOSEBERRY AND ELDERFLOWER CREAM

The Harborne area of Birmingham was once famous for the growing of gooseberries; the annual dinner of the Gooseberry Growers' Society was first held in Harborne in 1815. This recipe uses gooseberries to make a delicious light and fluffy dessert.

> 500g/1½ lbs gooseberries
> 30ml/2 tablespoonfuls elderflower cordial
> 300ml/10fl oz double cream
> 115g/4oz icing sugar

Place the gooseberries in a heavy saucepan, cover and cook over a low heat, shaking the pan occasionally until the gooseberries are tender. Tip the gooseberries into a bowl, crush them with a heavy wooden spoon or potato masher, then leave them to cool completely. (The gooseberries can be sieved or puréed if a finer consistency is preferred.)

Beat the cream until soft peaks form, then fold in half the crushed gooseberries. Sweeten with icing sugar to taste, and add the elderflower cordial. Sweeten the remaining gooseberries with icing sugar to taste.

Put a layer of the cream mixture in four dessert dishes or tall glasses, and then a layer of crushed gooseberries, then cover and chill for at least one hour before serving.

Pikelets, or pyclets if you prefer, are popular all over the Midlands, but the argument over whether they are the same thing as crumpets, and whether or not they should be cooked in a metal ring to contain the batter, seems to be a question of your own family tradition. However, for many people it is crumpets that are cooked with the batter contained in a special metal ring on the pan or griddle, and pikelets which are cooked as spoonfuls of batter dropped on to the pan or griddle – thus pikelets are thinner than crumpets, and are not cooked into an even round shape, as crumpets are. Whether you call them pikelets or crumpets, the top surface of these yeasted doughy delicacies becomes covered with holes during the cooking process. When you spread them with butter, hot from the pan, the melted butter oozes into the holes – perfect for winter teatimes!

RECIPE

PIKELETS

This recipe uses dried yeast, but if you can find fresh yeast, use 15g/
½ oz and cream it with a little sugar and some of the warmed water,
then leave in a warm place to activate and go frothy before using.
This quantity makes about 12 pikelets.

> 450g/1 lb plain flour (strong white breadmaking flour is best)
> 350ml/12 fl oz milk, warmed
> 350ml/12 fl oz water, warmed
> 7g/ ¼ oz powdered dried yeast (about one small sachet of dried
>   breadmaking yeast)
> 2 level teaspoonfuls salt
> 1 teaspoonful caster sugar
> 1 level teaspoonful baking powder
> A little sunflower or vegetable oil for greasing the pan or griddle

Place the flour, sugar and dried yeast into a bowl and make a well in
the centre. Pour in the warmed water and milk (add the yeast mixture
now, if using fresh yeast). Gradually stir the flour into the liquid until
you have a creamy batter with no lumps, and beat it well. Cover the
bowl with cling film and leave in a warm place for at least an hour
until the batter has risen and is bubbly.

Lightly grease a frying pan or griddle (and crumpet rings if using),
and place on a medium to high heat. Whisk the salt and the
baking powder into the batter. When the pan is hot, drop a good
tablespoonful of the mixture into the pan and cook for about five
minutes, or if using crumpet rings, place a ring in the pan and drop
in enough mixture to fill to just below the top. Lots of holes should
form on the surface of the pikelet as it cooks – if not, the mixture
is too thick, so whisk some more water into the batter mix before
making more. Cook the pikelet on one side for about 5 minutes until
the surface is just set, then flip it over (or take it out of the ring and
turn it) and cook the other side for about 2 minutes, until it is golden.
When each pikelet is cooked, remove it from the pan and keep
warm whilst you cook the rest of the batter. Either eat at once whilst
they are hot, spread with butter, or cool on a wire tray and keep for
toasting later.

WALSALL, THE BRIDGE 1967 W161022

COVENTRY, ST MARY'S HALL
1892 30929

RECIPE

COVENTRY GODCAKES

A 'godcake' is sometimes used in Warwickshire and West Midlands as a name for the triangle of grass at a road junction that is created as the road splits to go left and right. The name refers to the triangular-shaped pastry cakes known as Godcakes which were traditionally given by godparents in the Coventry area to their godchildren on New Year's Eve, for good luck. The child received both a blessing and a cake from the godparent, but the size of the cakes could vary, depending on the wealth and generosity of the giver!

225g/8oz puff pastry
115g/4oz mincemeat
1 egg white, beaten
2 teaspoonfuls rum or brandy (optional)
Caster sugar

Pre-heat the oven to 220°C/425°F/Gas Mark 7.

Roll out the pastry thinly on a lightly floured surface. Cut the pastry into 10cm (4 inch) squares, then cut each square in half on the diagonal to produce two triangles.

Mix the mincemeat with the rum or brandy if used, then place a small spoonful of mincemeat in the middle of half the pastry triangles – don't be too generous with the mixture or it will spill out from the sides of the cakes when the 'lids' are added. Moisten the edges of the triangles with a little water, then cover each filled triangle with a second triangle on top, pressing down firmly to seal the edges.

Cut three small diagonal slashes across the top of each Godcake with a sharp knife (some traditions say that these represent the Holy Trinity of Christian belief), then brush the top of each cake with beaten egg white and sprinkle with caster sugar. Place the Godcakes on a greased baking sheet and bake for about 15 minutes, or until golden and well puffed up. Cool on a wire rack and eat as soon as possible!

FRANCIS FRITH

PIONEER VICTORIAN PHOTOGRAPHER

Francis Frith, founder of the world-famous photographic archive, was a complex and multi-talented man. A devout Quaker and a highly successful Victorian businessman, he was philosophical by nature and pioneering in outlook. By 1855 he had already established a wholesale grocery business in Liverpool, and sold it for the astonishing sum of £200,000, which is the equivalent today of over £15,000,000. Now in his thirties, and captivated by the new science of photography, Frith set out on a series of pioneering journeys up the Nile and to the Near East.

INTRIGUE AND EXPLORATION

He was the first photographer to venture beyond the sixth cataract of the Nile. Africa was still the mysterious 'Dark Continent', and Stanley and Livingstone's historic meeting was a decade into the future. The conditions for picture taking confound belief. He laboured for hours in his wicker dark-room in the sweltering heat of the desert, while the volatile chemicals fizzed dangerously in their trays. Back in London he exhibited his photographs and was 'rapturously cheered' by members of the Royal Society. His reputation as a photographer was made overnight.

VENTURE OF A LIFE-TIME

By the 1870s the railways had threaded their way across the country, and Bank Holidays and half-day Saturdays had been made obligatory by Act of Parliament. All of a sudden the working man and his family were able to enjoy days out, take holidays, and see a little more of the world.

With typical business acumen, Francis Frith foresaw that these new tourists would enjoy having souvenirs to commemorate their days out. For the next thirty years he travelled the country by train and by pony and trap, producing fine photographs of seaside resorts and beauty spots that were keenly bought by millions of Victorians. These prints were painstakingly pasted into family albums and pored over during the dark nights of winter, rekindling precious memories of summer excursions. Frith's studio was soon supplying retail shops all over the country, and by 1890 F Frith & Co had become the greatest specialist photographic publishing company in the world, with over 2,000 sales outlets, and pioneered the picture postcard.

FRANCIS FRITH'S LEGACY

Francis Frith had died in 1898 at his villa in Cannes, his great project still growing. By 1970 the archive he created contained over a third of a million pictures showing 7,000 British towns and villages.

Frith's legacy to us today is of immense significance and value, for the magnificent archive of evocative photographs he created provides a unique record of change in the cities, towns and villages throughout Britain over a century and more. Frith and his fellow studio photographers revisited locations many times down the years to update their views, compiling for us an enthralling and colourful pageant of British life and character.

We are fortunate that Frith was dedicated to recording the minutiae of everyday life. For it is this sheer wealth of visual data, the painstaking chronicle of changes in dress, transport, street layouts, buildings, housing and landscape that captivates us so much today, offering us a powerful link with the past and with the lives of our ancestors.

Computers have now made it possible for Frith's many thousands of images to be accessed almost instantly. The archive offers every one of us an opportunity to examine the places where we and our families have lived and worked down the years. Its images, depicting our shared past, are now bringing pleasure and enlightenment to millions around the world a century and more after his death.

For further information visit: **www.francisfrith.com**

INTERIOR DECORATION

Frith's photographs can be seen framed and as giant wall murals in thousands of pubs, restaurants, hotels, banks, retail stores and other public buildings throughout Britain. These provide interesting and attractive décor, generating strong local interest and acting as a powerful reminder of gentler days in our increasingly busy and frenetic world.

FRITH PRODUCTS

All Frith photographs are available as prints and posters in a variety of different sizes and styles. In the UK we also offer a range of other gift and stationery products illustrated with Frith photographs, although many of these are not available for delivery outside the UK – see our web site for more information on the products available for delivery in your country.

THE INTERNET

Over 100,000 photographs of Britain can be viewed and purchased on the Frith web site. The web site also includes memories and reminiscences contributed by our customers, who have personal knowledge of localities and of the people and properties depicted in Frith photographs. If you wish to learn more about a specific town or village you may find these reminiscences fascinating to browse. Why not add your own comments if you think they would be of interest to others? See **www.francisfrith.com**

PLEASE HELP US BRING FRITH'S PHOTOGRAPHS TO LIFE

Our authors do their best to recount the history of the places they write about. They give insights into how particular towns and villages developed, they describe the architecture of streets and buildings, and they discuss the lives of famous people who lived there. But however knowledgeable our authors are, the story they tell is necessarily incomplete.

Frith's photographs are so much more than plain historical documents. They are living proofs of the flow of human life down the generations. They show real people at real moments in history; and each of those people is the son or daughter of someone, the brother or sister, aunt or uncle, grandfather or grandmother of someone else. All of them lived, worked and played in the streets depicted in Frith's photographs.

We would be grateful if you would give us your insights into the places shown in our photographs: the streets and buildings, the shops, businesses and industries. Post your memories of life in those streets on the Frith website: what it was like growing up there, who ran the local shop and what shopping was like years ago; if your workplace is shown tell us about your working day and what the building is used for now. Read other visitors' memories and reconnect with your shared local history and heritage. With your help more and more Frith photographs can be brought to life, and vital memories preserved for posterity, and for the benefit of historians in the future.

Wherever possible, we will try to include some of your comments in future editions of our books. Moreover, if you spot errors in dates, titles or other facts, please let us know, because our archive records are not always completely accurate—they rely on 140 years of human endeavour and hand-compiled records. You can email us using the contact form on the website.

Thank you!

For further information, trade, or author enquiries
please contact us at the address below:

**The Francis Frith Collection, Unit 6, Oakley Business Park,
Wylye Road, Dinton, Wiltshire SP3 5EU England.**
Tel: +44 (0)1722 716 376 Fax: +44 (0)1722 716 881
e-mail: sales@francisfrith.co.uk **www.francisfrith.com**